Praise for Rembrandt's Nose:

Imagine what might happen when an accomplished poet with a pitch-perfect ear immerses himself in the life and work of one of the West's great visual artists, and you will begin to know what it is to be carried away by Charles Wyatt's *Rembrandt's Nose*. In this volume, consisting of ekphrastic poems punctuated by lyric interludes and footnoted by inventories of Rembrandt's possessions auctioned off in a bankruptcy agreement, his famously prominent nose serves as a trope for the sights, smells, sounds, and appetites that made up the world of his perceptions. Wyatt's project is to restore all these items to their place in a life: the young artist drawing his first wife Saskia in a wide-brimmed straw hat, the ever-curious artist etching a rat poison peddler, the artist casting a cold eye on himself in the many self-portraits that chronicle his aging. The artworks themselves, described with sensitivity to both the dark and the light of the affections, become the vehicle through which the reader sees "in his, our own eyes" and comes to feel anew the wonder of being alive and sentient.

– Lee Sharkey, author of *Walking Backwards*

Rembrandt's Nose celebrates the mystery of art even while demystifying it. An accomplished musician, Wyatt has composed a "score" of three distinct voices that bring Rembrandt to life with sharp and startling immediacy. The first documents the bankruptcy that forced the artist to sell off his large personal collection. The second is a series of meditations on specific works by Rembrandt. These take us into the artist's mind, looking over his shoulder, sharing his thoughts: "He's looking for something new: / a hat, sword, feather, / but the nose is always / B-flat in the key of C." ("Twenty Self-Portraits"). A third voice, italicized and untitled, is that of Wyatt himself, a lyric commentary on the artist he admires from the distance of more than three centuries and whose triumphs and failures he has researched so diligently: Oh, nose, nose of Rembrandt, ancient hand weapons, / etchings, of Cranach, Raphael, Mantegna, Durer, / Titian, thirty volumes of sketches by Rembrandt / himself – Oh nose, eyes, old face in the moon. This inventive polyphonic play invites us to ask profound questions about the relationship of art to artist and of artist to life, "How much it costs to see." Notable is the poignant relationship with his first wife, Saskia, who died before thirty after childbirth: "she has an earache, / or just a tied-on nightcap, / and it's dark around her face." The artist's ink rendering fails, by comparison, to capture the actual woman, the mystery of her subjectivity: "Hold her upside down / and you'll hear it better. / It's like mice in the cupboard, / that subtle sound. / Study her face again. / She's listening now" ("Saskia Sitting Up in Bed"). Turning the visual into music and fact into vision, *Rembrandt's Nose* is a rare blend of passionate intelligence and structural mastery. Like Rembrandt's legacy, it's a work of enduring value.

– Stan Sanvel Rubin, author of *There. Here.*

Rembrandt's Nose combines ekphrastic and lyric poetry to reveal what's beneath the surface of the painter's work and behind the eyes of those self-portraits, including smells, sounds, tastes, and tactility. Wonders and mysteries are found even in the humblest places: in chairs, brooms, feathers, dust motes, "cows pissing." And there, like a refrain: the nose, "that sackbut, that viol, that harmonious bagpipe" – herald of imperfection, irony, appetite, and mortality. The mundane world also abides in the framing of the poems with lists of Rembrandt's belongings compiled in petitioning for voluntary bankruptcy. There's an echo throughout of Auden's remark about paintings of the Old Masters: "That even the dreadful martyrdom must run its course / Anyhow in a corner / some untidy spot / Where the dogs go on with their doggy life and the torturer's horse / scratches its innocent behind on a tree." This is a book to read and reread.

– William Trowbridge, author of Vanishing Points

The editors of Ex Ophidia Press Prize for Poetry have awarded a book that is as deeply moving as it is profound. Charles Wyatt's poems offer us a close study of Rembrandt's paintings, his pen and ink drawings and his black chalk drawings while succeeding in exciting a deeper understanding of ourselves.

Among the many lines I will forever call up are these from "The Amstel Dike near Trompenburg":

> – the frame we carry everywhere – think of
> that edge of thought, the book, the room,
> the square windowpane, the eye's fading
>
> periphery, the world's – somewhere between
> a man's horizon and his soul, the line
> he draws, and stays behind, over and again.

This book is, as Wyatt writes of Rembrandt's black chalk drawing "Standing Beggar," "something / drawn to flurry, / begging to exist."

After you read the poems and learn about Rembrandt's supplies and his furnishings, you will feel as deeply as Wyatt does in "Manoah's Sacrifice":

> Everything that isn't bolted down
> is blown away,
> every line, curved and tangled like wire,
> every splash of ink,
> is blown and flying off.

And so you will come to realize, as Wyatt writes in "The Good Samaritan Arriving at the Inn":

> it's not what you see that draws you.
> It's where you've been.

Rembrandt's Nose, with its unique approach to evoking the life of a master and his art, is an important reading experience.

– Sheila Bender, author of Behind Us the Way Grows Wider

Winner of the Second Annual
EX OPHIDIA PRESS PRIZE FOR POETRY
2017

Also by Charles Wyatt

Goldberg-Variations
Angelicus ex Machina
Myomancy
A Girl Sleeping
Swan of Tuonela
Falling Stones: the Spirit Autobiography of S.M. Jones
Listening to Mozart

Rembrandt's Nose

A handgun, a pistol
An old-fashioned powder flask
A Turkish powder flask
33 antique handguns and wind instruments
60 Indian guns, as well as arrows, shafts, javelins and bows
A small metal cannon

A catapult
13 items: arrows, bows, shields, etc.
4 catapults and longbows

Two iron helmets
An Attic helmet
An iron cuirass with a helmet
An iron shield by Quentin de Smet with unusual decoration
An osier shield
An iron gorget
5 antique hats and shields
20 halberds, broadswords and Indian fans
A giant's casque
5 cuirasses

An ebony frame
A gilded frame
One lot of paper, very large format

A small column
A cabinet with medals
A few curiosities, viz. pots and Venetian glasses
A small tric-trac board
A marble writing set

A box with minerals
47 items of marine as well as terrestrial fauna
A large quantity of horns, marine plants, casts from life
and many other curiosities
A large piece of white coral
A drawer containing a bird of paradise and six fans
A lot consisting of antlers
9 gourds and bottles
A large marine plant
The skins of a lion and a lioness

Rembrandt's Nose

POEMS BY
Charles Wyatt

EX OPHIDIA PRESS
Port Townsend, Washington
2018

Copyright © 2018 by Charles Wyatt

All rights reserved.
First edition.

Richard-Gabriel Rummonds, publisher and editor.
Sharon Cumberland, editor.
Gregory C. Richter, editor.
John D. Wagner, public relations and marketing.
Bradley Hutchinson, typesetting.
Manufactured in the United States of America.

Published by Ex Ophidia Press
724 Tyler Street, #3
Port Townsend, WA 98368

Some of these poems were published in
slightly different versions in the following publications.
See the List of Acknowledgements on page 83.

Wyatt, Charles
  Rembrandt's Nose / Charles Wyatt

Paperback ISBN 978-0-692-99541-9
Paperback ISBN 0692995412

For Cindy

Contents

Preface   xiii

Rembrandt's Nose   3
Portrait of Saskia in a Straw Hat   4
Twenty Self-Portraits   5
Judas Returning the Thirty Pieces of Silver   6
Standing Beggar   7
So much like a potato, Rembrandt's eyes   8
Old Man with His Arms Extended   9
The Entombment   10
Self-Portrait in a Cap, with Eyes Wide Open   11
There in the room with a mirror he must have kept   12
Christ Walking on the Waves   13
The Rat-Poison Peddler   14
Judith's Servant Puts Holofernes' Head into a Sack   15
a nose like a dead bird   16
Young Woman at Her Toilet   17
Study for an Adoration of the Magi   18
The Naughty Child   19
like a potato, Rembrandt's nose the tops   20
Three Women Looking Out from an Open Door   21
Woman with a Child Frightened by a Dog   22
Rembrandt shaving hot towel razor scraping   23
Farmhouse in Sunlight   24
Woman Seated in an Armchair with Her Head Resting
    on Her Left Hand   25
Mars and Venus Caught in a Net and Exposed by Vulcan
    to the Assembled Gods   26
Woman in North Holland Costume   27
a sneeze, a yawn, cows pissing   28
Manoah's Sacrifice   29
(Study for a) Portrait of Maria Tripp   30
Saskia Sitting Up in Bed   31

Self-Portrait Leaning on a Stone Sill   32
Saskia a sweet girl at the end   33
The Entombment, over a Sketch of an Executioner   34
Portrait Bust of a Lady in a Cap Plumed with an
    Ostrich Feather   35
The Good Samaritan Arriving at the Inn   36
Saskia a sweet girl at the end   37
Jacob and Rachel Listening to an Account of Joseph's
    Dreams   38
Cottage near the Entrance to a Wood   39
Seated Old Woman in a Large Headdress, Half-length,
    Turned to the Right   40
Young Man Pulling a Rope   41
Rembrandt's lost shadow drawings his faint   42
Young Man Pulling a Rope (Reprise)   43
Saint Jerome beside a Pollard Willow   44
on the walls Rembrandt's smoke drawings   45
Beggar Couple with Children and a Dog   46
A Dog Lying on the Ground with a Collar around His Neck   47
Christ Awakening the Apostles on the Mount of Olives   48
The Singel in Amersfoort   49
View across the IJ from the Dieman Dike   50
ravening springs / silence takes a bite   51
Winter Landscape   52
The Amstel Dike near Trompenburg   53
Farmhouse with a Water Mill amidst Trees   54
old man in the mirror he sees who, who it is   55
A Farmhouse among Trees   56
Lion Resting, Turned to the Left   57
Homer Reciting His Verses   58
Through the years   59
The Washing of the Feet   60
The Artist's Studio   61
The Descent from the Cross by Torchlight   62
Oh nose, nose of Rembrandt   63
Abraham's Sacrifice   64

Woman Looking out of a Window   65
A Coach   66
The Skeleton Rider   67
A Girl Sleeping   69
Sleeping Woman at a Window   70
Jael Driving a Nail into the Head of Sisera   71
Christ and the Woman Taken in Adultery   72
Self-Portrait at an Easel   73
Self-Portrait as Saint Paul   74
In 1662 sold Saskia's grave in the chancel   75
Self-Portrait with Brushes, Maulstick, and Palette in Hand   76
Self-Portrait in a Turban   77
Old man in the mirror, sitting today in the room   78
Self-Portrait as Democritus   79
Self-Portrait, Hands Clasped   80
Now it's lost in the moon, stags' horns   81

List of Acknowledgements   83
Resources   84
About the Author   87

Preface

Drawn up by the secretary of the Insolvency Court, with Rembrandt's help, on July 25 and 26, 1656. The document was an appendix to Rembrandt's petition to the States General for *cessio bonorum*, a form of voluntary bankruptcy, which offered the petitioner a measure of protection from his creditors.

The locations of the items in the house are as follows:

1. In the Vestibule
2. In the Reception Room
3. In the Family Living Room/Bedroom
4. In the Back Bedroom
5. In the Gallery of Curios
6. On a Shelf in the Back
7. The Books and Art Portfolios and Albums
8. In the Foyer Adjacent to the Gallery of Curios
9. The Small Studio for Rembrandt's Students
10. In Rembrandt's Studio
11. On the Picture Rack
12. In the Small Office
13. In the Basement Kitchen
14. In the Corridor
15. Linen at the Laundry
16. In the First Attic Room
17. In the Second Attic Room

Rembrandt's Nose

Here is a book of drawings, etchings, and paintings, most sold at auction. Some have been lost, then found again. Is out of sight lost? If so, they are all lost here again. Rembrandt's nose can't help appearing in the mirror. Nor can these echoes. The house is never empty. Somewhere there is a room of portraits, a room of landscapes, a room of scenes from common life, and in the room of histories, a life of Christ among other stories. And the ghost watches. We see in his, our own eyes.

Rembrandt's Nose

*

*He must have kept his costumes there in the room
with the mirror, the hats with feathers like the antennae
of creatures living under a stone, fabulous moths
or dragonfly nymphs, sand or gravel settled
and sealed over the only passage out – still,
darkness always finds a way to give itself
up to light, the water flowing, the noise of it
splashing against rocks, more feathers of foam –*

*Look at him there, the bags under his eyes,
staring at himself again as even the sky
sags over him, a moon floating up like
that thing under the stone –*

                    old man, old nose,
*quill pen scratching, mouse in the corner, birdsnest
tangle – but of what, lines worn into flourishes,
weed knots, rose vines trodden underfoot, crosshatch
crossings, and his nose always there in the middle,
but not quite, looking like he slung it over
his shoulder, so much like a potato, Rembrandt's nose –*

Portrait of Saskia in a Straw Hat

*This is drawn after my wife, when
she was 21 years old, the third day after our betrothal,
the 8th of June 1633.*

Of course, we should see her in her wide brimmed hat,
the fingers of one hand touching her face,
the other clutching a wilted flower.

Take my word, she's appealing, virginal –
her eyes are thoughtful, a shade dreamy.
Her little mouth is touching, a child's mouth.

She's not this pretty in real life by half I'll guess,
and she's leaning, resting her elbows on something.
He'll draw her like this often –

in bed, at the window, having her hair done.
She doesn't seem inclined to bustle about.
She's pretty enough though, and wealthy, too.

Years later, and this is the sad part,
you can see it in his face afterward,
in those amazing self-portraits,

he'll take her from the large book
bound in black leather, silverpoint on white vellum,
and sell her at auction to pay his debts.

Twenty Self-Portraits
Etchings.
1628–1631

The hair seems sometimes
more detailed than life,
etched strand by strand.
Larger than life, that's it –

For a frown, a frowse;
wild curls for shadow.
There he is, there again.

He's looking for something new:
a hat, sword, feather,
but the nose is always
B-flat in the key of C.

And one thing more, the eyes,
like faces we've all made
for mirrors, smile or sneer –

however turned the skull,
the eyes can't help showing,
locked as they are upon themselves,
how much it costs to see.

Judas Returning the Thirty Pieces of Silver
Pen and brush, brown and gray inks.
c. 1629

Out of the darkest wood
an invisible wing unfolds,
drawn to an unlit flame.

Coins must clink and fall in light.
Judas, the kneeling figure,
has no face.

The shapes of stones surround him
in a surf of darkness.
"What does this mean?"

they all seem to ask.
Above them the bare wall –
behind it, the dark world.

———

1. In the Vestibule
   One small painting of a pastry cook by Adriaen Brouwer.
   One painting of card players by the same.
   One painting of a woman and child by Rembrandt.
   One painting of an artist's studio by Brouwer.
   One painting of a magnificent spread of food by the same.
   One wing in plaster, invisible.
   One statue of two naked children cast in plaster.
   One sleeping child cast in plaster.
   One shabby shoe.

Standing Beggar
Black chalk.
c. 1629

These lines demand,
hands on hips,
toes turned out,
each boot a rock
of certainty.

At the right side,
(his left) toward which
his eyes darken,
scribble meets air.

He's girdled in the same,
darker if anything.
And inside his arm
I see, perched on
an insouciant crosshatch,

a bird, not
a real bird, but something
drawn to flurry,
begging to exist.

———

One small painting of a landscape by Rembrandt.
Another painting of a landscape by the same.
One painting of a standing woman by the same.
One painting of the Nativity of Christ by Jan Lievens.
One painting of St. Jerome by Rembrandt.
One small painting of dead hares by the same.
One small painting of a hog by the same.
One small painting of a landscape by Hercules Seghers.
One painting of a landscape by Lievens.
Another with a perching bird by the same.
One small painting of a landscape by Rembrandt.

*

So much like a potato, Rembrandt's eyes –
cornea, iris, pupil, the caruncula lachrymalis
at each corner, lids curtained, drooping, bulging,
lashes like weeds along the Amstel, eyebrows
superciliary, hands and feet, chins, faces –
not to neglect the oiliness of a prosperous nose,
folds of a jowl or wattle overlapping / one
eye always looking forward, but nose
from memory / onthouden *to recollect:*
a pike's tail spit-roasted, from memory,
a carp simmered in Rhenish, pinked
with its own blood, anchovies and verjus
of unripe grapes or the famous pie
of boned birds, each nesting within
the next: heron swan capon wild goose
pintail widgeon shoveller duck lapwing
pigeon plover woodcock snipe lark –
Oh nose, nesting nose, and from memory.

Old Man with His Arms Extended
Black chalk.
c. 1629

After the woodthrush calls,
and not during,
can his song take shape.

But where is a shrug
a shrug?

This old man is draped
like a circus tent.
His hands palm heaven.

He has no feet.
Neither does a mountain,
which seldom gestures

under its scribbling of trees.

———

One painting of fighting lions by Rembrandt.
One painting of a landscape in moonlight by Jan Lievens.
One portrait painting by Rembrandt.
Another portrait painting by the same.
One horizontal painting of a still life retouched by Rembrandt.
One soldier in armor with his arms extended by the same.
One vanitas with a skull retouched by the same.
Another vanitas with a scepter retouched by the same.
One painting of a seascape by Hendrick van Anthonissen.
Four Spanish chairs covered with Russian leather.
Two Spanish chairs with black cushions.
One pine step stool.

The Entombment
Red chalk, heightened with white.
1630

Like the folds of a curtain
seen through themselves
beneath an angel's faint wings,
all these shapes struggle,
growing as we watch.
The body has sunk into a leaden arch.

Backs bent and feet slipping,
the living labor on. Still,
there is no sound but breathing –
and the wings above are tall,
shaped like the flame of a candle.

---

2. In the Reception Room
   One painting of the Good Samaritan retouched by Rembrandt.
   One painting of a rich man by Palma Vecchio, of which Pieter de la Tombe owns a half share.
   One backyard with angels by Rembrandt.
   One painting of two greyhounds from life by the same.
   One large painting of the Descent from the Cross by the same with a handsome gold frame.
   One painting of the Raising of Lazarus by the same.
   One painting of a courtesan doing her hair by the same.
   One painting of a small wooded landscape by Hercules Seghers.

Self-Portrait in a Cap, with Eyes Wide Open
Etching and drypoint.
1630

This is the young Rembrandt
whose face still contains his nose
practicing his scales
at the mirror.
Anger, astonishment, alarm –

faint mustache riding
that bassoon embouchure
in disbelief,
a clinging mayfly,

little more than ambient
cross hatching,
but the eyes are wide.
A high shoulder,

eyebrows drawn up
with a single purse string –
the effect perfect,
a chord so slightly,

so carefully
out of tune,
it shimmers on the page.

———

One painting of Tobias by Pieter Lastman.
One painting of the Raising of Lazarus by Jan Lievens.
One painting of a mountainous landscape by Rembrandt.
One small painting of a landscape by Govert Janszoon.
Two portrait paintings by Rembrandt.
One bassoon by Lievens.
Two paintings in tones of gray by Jan Porcellis.
One portrait painting by Rembrandt.
One portrait painting by Adriaen Brouwer.
One painting of a view from the dunes in tones of gray by Porcellis.

*

*There in the room with a mirror he must have kept
his costumes, hats with feathers like the antennae
of creatures living under a stone, sand
or gravel in a stream, a sealed passage
to get out, float in the current or swim to the surface,
bags under his eyes as the sky sags over,
moon floating up like that thing under the stone,
old men, old noses, quill pen, scratching
sounds, birdsnest tangle, scrim of weed knot,
lines crossing like rose vines trodden underfoot,
his nose always there in the middle but not quite,
looking like he slung it over his shoulder.*

*Now in his walks along the Amstel, the tops
of the grass fine and fluting, making that harsh noise
when he drags his feet and the birds fly up in clusters,
he sees how a bird's chest heaves out, the whole of it
fat with song, song hung like a heart
over the spine and ribs as if the air
it figured were alive –*

Christ Walking on the Waves
Pen and brown ink.
c. 1632–33

We know that waves heave up
and drop away, that our eyes
can't frame anything like this.

But it's there – the boat's wood bow
high as a water tower with an anchor
strapped on to remind us what it is
is in the top right-hand corner

poking clear out of the frame.
This sketch might be dripping water –

it's been done quickly enough,
but the story is the thing,
and the idea was to try out Jesus

in the lower left, let him reach down
to a chap who's half sunk –
design is one thing, faith another.

———

One small painting of a view from the dunes in tones of gray
    by Jan Porcellis.
One small painting of a hermit by Jan Lievens.
Two small portrait paintings by Lucas van Valckenborch.
One small painting of a stockade on fire by Jacopo Bassano.
One painting of a charlatan after Adriaen Brouwer.
Two portrait paintings by Jan Pynas.
One painting of a view in perspective by Lucas van Leyden.
One paintng of a priest after Lievens.
One small study of a drowning model by Rembrandt.

The Rat-Poison Peddler
Etching.
1632

Here's a peasant with a tub fixed to a tall stick,
dead rats hung from it, and more improbably,
live ones, one on his shoulder, one atop the tub.
He has a tall hat, too. A sword hangs from his side.

His helper, perhaps a dwarf, holds a wire cage,
and the turbaned householder reaches out from his door
a coin or two. A broken barrel decorates the foreground.
The village and trees recede delicately behind.
The shoulder rat (a pet or half-poisoned?)

has the only sweet face in this tableau,
and from under the wooden arch that caps the doorway –
darkness, the smell of onions, damp stone, ashes.

One small painting of a shepherd and his flock by Rembrandt.
One drawing by the same.
One painting of the Flagellation of Christ by the same.
One painting in tones of gray by Jan Porcellis.
One painting in tones of gray by Simon de Vlieger.
One small painting of a landscape by Rembrandt.
One portrait painting of a woman from life by the same.
One portrait painting by Raphael.
One painting of houses from life by Rembrandt.
One painting of a landscape from nature by the same.
One painting of some small houses by Hercules Seghers.

Judith's Servant Puts Holofernes' Head into a Sack
Pen and ink.
c. 1632–34

We might have dreamed these lines.
It is all so swift, the head
should not have fallen,

yet there it is
at the bottom.
Perhaps she's holding it down.

Judith staggers with her sword.
Soon she's going to fall.
Her servant's got

the darkest lines
and Holofernes' head.
The rest of Holofernes

tends to float,
is delicate, a splash of blood
become an angel's wing.

———

One painting of the goddess Juno by Jan Pynas.
One mirror in an ebony frame.
One ebony frame.
One marble wine cooler.
One head in a sack.
One walnut table with a Tournai damask tablecloth.
Seven Spanish chairs with green velvet cushions.

*

a nose like a dead bird
remembering its song, a thin kind of rhythm
ambling behind wide spaced ribs – just
enough architecture to hold the morning –
still – (and still is what's under it)
everything has its own song, even Rembrandt's
nose, that sackbut, that viol, that harmonious bagpipe –
pastei of finches boiled with sugar
And pine nuts hidden beneath a golden crust,
A bream stuffed with its own roe
And sharpened with mace, calf's-tongue tart
(oh nose) with sugar and ginger

Young Woman at Her Toilet
Pen and brush, brown and gray inks.
c. 1632–34

An old woman braids her hair
behind a cloud of wash.

There's enough light
in her seated form

to wake the world.
The girl sits, hands in her lap.

The old woman twists and tugs
while one braid

and a flight of swallows
slide down the front.

---

3. In the Family Living Room/Bedroom
   One painting of Jephthah by Pietro Testa.
   One painting of the Madonna and Child by Rembrandt.
   One young woman at her toilet by the same.
   One painting of the Crucifixion of Christ by the same.
   One painting of a naked woman by the same.
   One copy of a painting after Annibale Carracci.
   Two paintings of half-length figures by Adriaen Brouwer.
   Another copy of a painting after Carracci.
   One small painting of a seascape by Jan Porcellis.
   One character painting of an old man by Jan van Eyck.
   One posthumous portrait of a deceased man by Abraham Vincks

Study for an Adoration of the Magi
Pen and brown ink.
c. 1634–35

In the night a moth makes these lines,
coiling into the dark
before resting on my window.

First, this flowery ellipse, then
the next – just so, in order
from first to last.

Now the child held before me,
and I wonder as I was meant to wonder,
the light sweeping around me.

I am a stone in its stream,
and I was drawn myself,
all my separate wanderings,

and all the dark places where
I might have disappeared.

One painting of the Resurrection of the Dead by Aert van Leyden.
One sketch of a moth circling by Rembrandt.
One copy of a sketch after the same.
Two portrait paintings from life by the same.
One painting of the Consecration of Solomon's Temple in tones of
    gray by the same.
One copy of a painting of the Circumcision of Christ after the same.
Two small paintings of landscapes by Hercules Seghers.
One gilt frame surrounding a damp stone.
One small oak table and one clothes horse.
One wardrobe and one oak press.
Four plain chairs with green cushions.
One copper kettle.

The Naughty Child
Pen and brush, brown ink, some white.
c. 1635

Terribly centered, this one.
And a big boy, already slipping
down, perhaps, effort
etched on his mother's brow.

What a tangle where she grabs him!
And he's sliding, squirming.
He's just dropped something
that hasn't landed yet.

Naughty child, indeed.
His yowls are heavy, even
his mother's clothes are helping
hold him up, those black shadows

offsetting. She'll have a sore back.
Still, (though he's not) he's
in the center of her world,
and she's no mind to cast him down.

---

4. In the Back Bedroom
   One small wooded landscape with badgers by an
     unknown master.
   One character painting of an old man by Rembrandt.
   One large painting of a landscape by Hercules Seghers.
   One character painting of a woman by Rembrandt.
   One Ganymede Carried Away by the Eagle of Zeus
     by the same.
   One painting of a view of a village by Govert Janszoon.
   One painting of a young ox from life by Rembrandt.
   One large painting of the Woman of Samaria by Giorgione,
     of which a half share belongs to de la Tombe.

*

*like a potato, Rembrandt's nose the tops
of the grass fine and fluting making that harsh
noise when he walks and bird clusters fly up –
bird's chest heaves out, song over the spine as if
the air it contained were alive, a nose
like a dead bird remembering its song –
everything has its own song even
Rembrandt's nose that sackbut that viol that bagpipe
harmonious /*

*Now nose in the outhouse: seventeenth century shit,
fatty pork, geese, onions, fresh bread,
ale, wine, wine like quail's blood, wine like
a certain blackbird's eye, like Saskia in silverpoint,
night soil traffickers,* vuilnisvaarders,
*sheep dung to the Amersfoort tobacco growers,
horse shit to the horticulturists for cabbage,
cole seeds beans turnips parsnips radishes
beets white carrots / in white mixed with
a minute quantity of black, a touch of verdigris,
the pupil never dead black but brown umber*

Three Women Looking Out from an Open Door

Brush, pen, and wash.
c. 1645

Of course, we join them, you and I,
who must stand deeper within the house.
Around us is the darkness of a theater,
and light plays on its stage of sky.

We see them framed in this inner gloom.
(The walls are thick in this old house.)
Two of the women sit, backs to us,
in the arched doorway, watching the world.

One nearly conceals the other, seated
as she is, near us, on a short chair.
The third stands amid her folds and drapes,
her face unfinished, a brush outline.

But we shouldn't mind, her body's
gesture is eloquent of interest.
What's outside? We want to ask them
as the light pours past like soft silver

from the street where someone stands,
perhaps bends slightly from the waist
like the standing woman nearest us,
and like us, bowing ever so slightly,

waiting for the next moment, a voice,
a sparrow's glint, someone come home at last.

Woman with a Child Frightened by a Dog

Pen and brown ink.
c. 1636

She's laid down her groceries –
The composition is a clock's face game.
There's the dog's nose pointing,
"Whippet with a long tail climbing stairs."
There's the kneeling woman,
arms around the child
who wears a "fall-down hat,"
like a helmet or a squash,
arms fending off the dog,
friendly, no doubt,
but the child's face is wrong.
This is almost a frown of interest.

And looking closer – child, mother, dog,
all squeeze into each other's space –
dog's nose in child's arm,
child into mother's mute embrace.
Above, from an open window,
(perhaps an afterthought)
a turbaned head looks out
indifferently. The dog's
the little hand at seven.
The big hand's turbaned dead on twelve,
and, hanging from the pendulum,
half a fat cabbage, drawn with love.

*

*Rembrandt shaving hot towel razor scraping
innocent as a shark (angels and noses
have no bones) soap lye scented the sky wide
clouds passing over those tangles of lines
listen to them where they are most knotted
and where they soar alone feathers of dust
in the corner / servant girl sweeping –
the dust flares flowers up, throws a hood
over its dark face, sparks from the broom*

*Rembrandt shaving: hot towel, razor scraping,
That sad little mustache, he remembers it, a whisper,
a mayfly standing too long on the water's skin,
until the dark, slower than rose vines, twines in –
soap, lye scented, the sky wide, clouds passing over
those tangles of lines – listen to them where
they are most knotted, and listen again where
they soar alone –*

Farmhouse in Sunlight
Pen and brush, brown ink.
c. 1636

If a tree can gather the sun,
this house is a forest,
and the light's a treasure
hidden already.

Bright shadows hold up
four chimneys,
and we're close enough
to be inside

where sharp lines
from the guarded windows
bind armies of morning dust
escaping an angry broom.

———

Three antique statues.
One sketch of the Entombment of Christ by Rembrandt.
One painting of St. Peter's Boat by Aert van Leyden.
One painting of the Resurrection of Christ by Rembrandt.
One painting of the Virgin Mary by Raphael.
One painting of the head of Christ by Rembrandt.
One small landscape with four chimneys by Abel Grimmer.
One painting of the Crucifixion of Christ by Lelio da Novellara.
Another painting of the head of Christ by Rembrandt.
One painting of a small ox by Pieter Lastman.
One small broom by the same.
One vanitas, retouched by Rembrandt.
One painting of an Ecce Homo in tones of gray by Rembrandt.

Woman Seated in an Armchair with Her Head Resting on Her Left Hand

Pen and bistre.
c. 1637–40

The chair's arm is a low one
so she's bending down to reach her hand
which we see at first,
knuckles just beneath her nose

which is rather large
because it's spread by the pressure
of the hand resting against her face
and by something like dejection.

Rembrandt has drawn a ring of curls
around her high forehead
which look like the leaves of trees
in his farmhouse landscapes.

Her eyes are closed, perhaps
in rest, but possibly in suffering –
No, I could not call it sleep
because the chair beneath

keeps moving, drawn as it is
in such violence – oh yes,
it holds her up and answers
to the laws of physics, but

reluctantly. See how the folds
of her robe are trembling.
She is like water, calm nearest
the point the wind is coming from,

but stirred into hatches and waves
on that far shore where the chair
is threatening to explode
the moment you turn away.

Mars and Venus Caught in a Net and Exposed by Vulcan to the Assembled Gods

Pen and bistre, wash.
c. 1638

Not cows in a field,
nor birds on a wire,
where there is room to munch,
space to ruffle a feather,

these gods are a pile of stones,
a mountainside – they're jammed
breast to belly, yet
assembled in a fine diagonal.

If it should rain gods
the fields would stink a week.
Earthworms would drown
and float forlornly,

smelling, however,
even when the sun came out
and swirled about its rays,
better than this bunch.

One painting of Abraham's Sacrifice by Jan Lievens.
One vanitas with worms, retouched by Rembrandt.
One pile of stones in grisaille by Hercules Seghers.
One painting of a sunset by Rembrandt.
One large mirror, hats with feathers like antennae.
Six chairs with blue cushions.
One oak table with an embroidered tablecloth.
One cedar clothes press.
One chest for children's napkins, ditto.
One bed and bolster with blue bed curtains.
Two pillows and two blankets.
One wicker chair.
One warming pan.

Woman in North Holland Costume
Pen and brush, brown ink.
c. 1638–40

Is she the nurse of Titus, son of Rembrandt,
De Minnemoer van Titus,
as an 18th-century hand, on the reverse,
asserts?

She is herself in reverse, revealing only
her broad back. A V of something like fur
points toward her waist, and the same thing,
brushed and spiked, is close around her neck.

She's done to a turn, brown ink, pen and brush,
and Titus, (if it be he) is behind the rail
where her left hand rests momentarily.
There might be a cloth, or a scarf, beneath it.

It's not important, and Titus, less so,
he's a squiggle. It looks like he's smoking
a pipe. Her skirt pleats are virtuoso scales.
There's an arch to frame her from the right.

She's saying, "Is this the best I get,
zoon van Rembrandt, my back for posterity?
Even in Dutch, it might be a joke.

―――

5. In the Gallery of Curios
   Two terrestrial globes.
   One small box containing minerals.
   One small column of feathers of foam.
   One small pewter pot.
   One statue of a child pissing.
   Two East Indian bowls and a third decorated with a Chinese man.
   One marble bust of an empress and another of the Emperor Augustus .
   One East Indian gunpowder flask .
   One East Indian cup and one lady's sewing basket.
   One cow pissing.
   One marble bust of the Emperor Caius and another of the Emperor
      Caligula.

a sneeze, a yawn, cows pissing –
Rembrandt is hungry today, has a plate of eggs
and bread, chews loudly in the dark, feathers
of dust in the corner, servant girl sweeping.
The dust flares flowers up, throws a hood
over its dark face, sparks from the broom
fail to ignite, its blunt and shabby straw
scraping wood smooth, warm suds on the stone stoop,
cows pissing –
      sneeze, a yawn, and other beggars:
loseneers *(escaped captives of the Turks)*
iuweeliers *(specialize in fake gems)*
swijgers *(smear themselves with horse shit and water*
to simulate jaundice) schleppers *(phony*
Catholic priests) nachbehuylers *(lie*
with their children in front of houses moaning
until they are let in –

Manoah's Sacrifice
Pen and brown ink.
c. 1639

There's an angel flushed up
like a roadside crow,
and it's all haste.
It's that scene in *Close Encounters*
where the UFO becomes a helicopter
and searchlights shine on startled faces.

Everything that isn't bolted down
is blown away,
every line, curved and tangled like wire,
every splash of ink,
is blown and flying off.

There *are* times when light shows through us,
when, in our amazement,
we become transparent.
Think of the noise an angel makes,
all that flapping.
They must always see our faces like this.

One pair of Roman leggings.
Two porcelain cassowaries from New Guinea.
One marble bust of Heraclitus.
Two small porcelain figurines.
One marble bust of the Emperor Nero.
Two iron helmets.
One Japanese helmet and one Carpathian helmet.
One marble bust of a Roman emperor and another of Faustina.
One Moor's head from life cast in bronze.
One marble bust of Socrates.
One marble bust of Homer and another of Aristotle.
One brown antique angel, astonished.
One iron coat of armor and a helmet.

(Study for a) Portrait of Maria Tripp
*Pen and brush, brown ink,
touches of red chalk, heightened with white.
c. 1639*

The looming behind those lit faces
must have a form,
like scaffolding to hold the moon.

And there's something
which will become a chair arm,
at and below her elbow.

In that lower right triangle
a Loch Ness monster splashes
toward her. He'll soon disappear.

Everything is as it will be
around her, but not yet tamed, darkened.
She'll grow mild and beautiful,

leaving only polished circles
of light on the chair arm,
a bracelet, pinching her wrist.

———

*One marble bust of the Emperor Galba.
One marble bust of the Emperor Otto.
One marble bust of the Emperor Vitellius.
One marble statue of the Emperor Vespasian.
One marble bust of the Emperor Titus Vespasianus.
One marble bust of the Emperor Domitian.
One marble bust of Brutus.
One ditto Loch Ness monster.
Forty-seven specimens of land and marine vegetation.
Twenty-three specimens of land and marine animals.
One hammock with two metal* kalbassen *(metal
    attachments in the shape of a gourd), one of copper.
Eight large pieces of various objects cast in plaster from life.*

Saskia Sitting Up in Bed
Pen and brush, brown ink.
c. 1639–40

Her bed is a Zen brush-stroke,
but she's where
she ought to be,
holding across her breast,
her lap,
a little nest of pen scratching.

She can't hear it.
she has an earache,
or just a tied-on nightcap,
and it's dark around her face.

Hold her upside down
and you'll hear it better.
It's like mice in the cupboard,
that subtle sound.
Study her face again.
She's listening now.

———

6. On a Shelf in the Back
   *A great quantity of shells and sea plants, cast in plaster from
       nature, and many other rarities.*
   One antique statue of Cupid.
   One handgun and a pistol.
   One steel shield decorated with figures by Quentin de Smet.
   One old-fashioned gunpowder flask and one Turkish gunpowder flask.
   One box containing medals.
   One padded shield.
   Two completely naked figures.
   One death mask of Prince Maurice cast in plaster from his own face.
   Two statues of a lion and a bull from life cast in plaster.
   Several walking sticks and one longbow.

Self-Portrait Leaning on a Stone Sill
Etching, drypoint, burin.
1639

In this large etching, the young man
tries on the masterful, gazes
out from under a rakish hat.

A huge sleeve drapes the wall –
insouciant folds compound and
drift like building clouds.

This is the grand style – hair
to broad shoulders curled
and keenly cut, strand by strand –

Brow wrinkled with fine thought,
mustache and beard trimmed
rakishly – the eyes are wise,

at least, appear so – this is a man
who's bought a house in the Breestraat,
a house so fine, so large,

nothing inside its walls could
ever fail – sign then, and large,
too, *Rembrandt made this, 1639.*

---

7. The Books, Art Portfolios, and Albums
    One portfolio of sketches by Rembrandt.
    One portfolio of engravings and woodcuts by Lucas van Leyden.
    One portfolio of woodcuts by Cornelis de Wael.
    One book containing shadows.
    *One portfolio of copperplate engravings by Francesco Vanni and others,
        including Federico Barocci.*
    One portfolio of copperplate engravings after Raphael.
    One small gilt bedstead modeled by Rombout Verhulst.
    *One portfolio of copperplate engravings by van Leyden with single and
        duplicate sheets.*
    One portfolio of drawings by the leading masters of the whole world.
    One portfolio of precious drawings by Andrea Mantegna.

*

*Saskia a sweet girl at the end
of a quill pen sometimes in silverpoint –
Along the dike marshes the riverbank
blackbirds / also windy that flat land
trees breathing the farmhouses like toadstools,
sun filling the wide spaces and shadow
under the trees the ear hears first what is
inside then the wind outside / sounds
of wagons rolling squeaking rehearsing echoes,
naked horses with bells and music of pipes
flute viols Rembrandt dancing –*

*Barking at the Monday dog market
shopping for* middags sallet *wild chicory
purslane burnet borage leaf
dent-de-lion buttercup catnip calendula
dried beans and peas gruel and bacon*

*call of the sharpeners and grinders
over the wind and the squeaking wagons
sabers and pikes, halberds and partizans
ice skates and picks, daggers and peat-diggers
razors and scalpels, saws and axes
along the Herengracht, the Keizersgracht
the Prinsengracht, wind, wide cloud shadow*

The Entombment, over a Sketch of an Executioner

Pen and brown ink.
c. 1640–41

Christ's head lolls back
and drips brown ink.
He has three right arms
and the figures holding him
are hopelessly entangled.

Given a half turn, (9 to 12),
a head and raised hands
appear at the level of the grave.
On the verso more clearly
this figure holds a sword

in a tight backswing prior
to beheading a kneeling man,
John the Baptist, we must assume –
economy and irony themselves
as near kin as cousins.

———

One large portfolio of drawings and prints by many masters.
Another larger portfolio of drawings and prints by various masters.
One portfolio of curious miniature drawings together with various woodcuts and copperplate engravings of various folk costumes.
One portfolio of prints of Pieter Bruegel the Elder.
One portfolio of engravings after Raphael.
One portfolio of very valuable engravings after the same.
One portfolio of prints by Antonio Tempesta.
One portfolio of woodcuts and copperplate engravings by Lucas Cranach.
One portfolio of prints by Annibale, Agostino, and Ludovico Carracci, Guido Reni, and Jusepe de Ribera.

Portrait Bust of a Lady in a Cap Plumed with an Ostrich Feather

Black chalk and wash.
c. 1640

And you'd swear she's done in oil,
posed in that window with a flash
of curtain at her left ear,

something like Redon's little
treasure pots of color at her elbow
or in the splash behind her head –

but she's mere smudged black chalk,
and her face is faint as a cloud.
She's had a sad day – and the master

has made her this way to tune your eye,
to make you want to improvise
a melody you'll always remember.

———

One portfolio of copperplate engravings and etchings of figures
    by Antonio Tempesta.
One large portfolio of the same.
Another of the same with various prints.
One portfolio of copperplate engravings of portraits by
    Hendrick Goltzius and Jan Muller.
One portfolio of very fine engravings after Raphael.
One portfolio of drawings by Adriaen Brouwer.
One very large portfolio of prints with nearly all the works of Titian.
Some rare items including pottery and Venetian glass.
One old portfolio with a series of sketches by Rembrandt.
One old portfolio.
One large book of jellyfish sketches by Rembrandt.

The Good Samaritan Arriving at the Inn
Pen and brush, brown ink, corrected with white.
c. 1641–43

It's dark now, but there's light inside,
horses drawn up like clouds over small trees –
all that bulk is comforting.
They're taking him in,
the poor man who was set upon by thieves,
then ignored by a priest and a Levite,
wounded and naked though he was.
There's a man on the steps lighting his pipe.
The Samaritan tends his horse still.
Think of that warm light inside.
Amsterdam or Jericho,
it's not what you see that draws you.
It's where you've been.

One empty portfolio.
One small tric-trac board.
One harpsichord and very antique chair.
One Chinese bowl containing minerals.
One large cluster of white coral.
One portfolio of copperplate engravings of statues.
One portfolio of the complete works of Maerten van Heemskerck.
One portfolio of drawings and prints after Anthony van Dyck,
    Peter Paul Rubens, and various other old masters.

*Saskia a sweet girl at the end
of a quill pen, sometimes in silverpoint, but always
lounging about –*
                *"this is drawn after my wife
when she was 21 years old, the third day
of our betrothal," years later, does he take her out,
virginal on parchment, thinking, how young and pretty –
Rumbartus, Cornelia, the second Cornelia – all dead
within a few months – only Titus now, but no
Saskia, gazing absently from window and bed,
once even with a toothache, a wealthy girl.*

*And the nursemaid Geertje, Geertje Dircx,
something odd about the girl.
but a man gets lonely, has his. . .
walks alone along the Amstel, his selves:
the soldier, the bourgeois, the prince,
the beggar, the master – gazing absently from
arm on the sill, resting on the wall, the will of cloth
brocade,* broccato, *twisted thread, a spike,*
brocchus, *a badger, arm insouciant*

Jacob and Rachel Listening to an Account of Joseph's Dreams

Pen and brush, brown ink, heightened with white.
c. 1642–43

>Oh where is the sweet young Rachel
>from the well at Haran?
>This Rachel has no teeth.
>She leans on the high back of Jacob's chair,
>and he, too, too old, leans to listen.
>The chair leans, we lean –
>Such dreams, such stories.
>We'll hear them again and again.
>We never tire of our dreams.

———

One portfolio of landscapes by various masters.
One portfolio of the work of Michelangelo.
Two small plaited baskets containing Rachel's dreams.
One portfolio of erotica after Raphael, Rosso Fiorentino,
  Annibale Carracci, and Giulio Bonasone.
One portfolio of landscapes by various esteemed masters.
One portfolio of woodcuts of Turkish buildings by Melchior Lorck,
  Hendrick van Aelst, and others depicting Turkish life and customs.
One East Indian basket containing various prints by Rembrandt,
  Wenzel Hollar. Hieronymus Cock, and others.
One album bound in black leather containing the best sketches
  by Rembrandt.

Cottage near the Entrance to a Wood
Pen and bistre, wash, some black and red chalk.
1644

A barrel on the porch,
and Grandma at the door
peering out like Saskia.
There's a room behind her
and a wood, heaped up
with shed roofs of wash and leaves.

The cottage is a drift of shadow,
blown up, hitched together,
comfortably disguised behind
that foreground log, an excuse
for an odd, atonal line,
leftover from a fairy binge.

———

One papiere kas *(cardboard box or paper folder) containing prints by Martin Schongauer, Holbein, Hans Brosamer, and Israhel van Meckenem.*
One portfolio of the complete etchings of Rembrandt.
One portfolio of drawings of naked men and women by the same.
One portfolio of drawings of all the celebrated buildings and views of Rome by all the most excellent masters.
One Chinese basket containing heads cast in plaster.
One empty album.
One ditto as above, but not entirely empty.
One papiere kas *containing the feathers of finches.*

Seated Old Woman in a Large Headdress, Half-Length, Turned to the Right
Black chalk.
c. 1643

She's not old because her eyes and cheeks are sunken,
nor because her chin falls sharply against her breast.
It's probably her mouth, compressed and knowing,
or the way she looks down when she might be looking up.

Her body, on the other hand, is filled with rapid strokes
of chalk – you can see how the master hurried
to get to her face, and as a result she looks as if
she might spring up, gather her skirts, and fly away.

One papiere kas *containing landscapes drawn from nature by Rembrandt.*
One portfolio of trial proofs by Pieter Paul Rubens and Jacob Jordaens.
One portfolio of portraits by Pieter van Mierevelt, Titian and others.
One small Chinese basket containing hellgrammites.
One portfolio of architectural prints.
One portfolio of drawings of animals from life by Rembrandt.
One portfolio of prints by Frans Floris, Willem Buyteweg, Hendrik Goltzius, and Abraham Bloemaert.
One packet of drawings of subjects from antiquity by Rembrandt.
Five small albums in quarto of drawings by the same.
One portfolio of prints of architectural views.

Young Man Pulling a Rope
Pen and brush, brown ink, heightened with white.
c. 1645

> In pen and brush and folds
> and bold outlines
> and bristling
> with the queer notion
> that light has weight
>
> and enough at that
> to sound the bell
> we cannot see
> which at this moment
> poses upside down
>
> waiting

One copy of Medea, *a tragedy by Jan Six.*
One copy of All Jerusalem *by Jacques Callot.*
One album bound in parchment of landscapes drawn from nature by Rembrandt.
One portfolio of figure sketches by the same.
One ditto containing sketches of bells.
One small album with wooden covers with sketches of circular plates.
One portfolio of views drawn by Rembrandt.
One portfolio of outstanding examples of calligraphy.
One portfolio of drawings of statues from life by Rembrandt.
Another portfolio of drawings of statues from life by the same.
One portfolio of pen and ink sketches by Pieter Lastman.
One portfolio of red chalk drawings by the same.

*

*Rembrandt's lost shadow drawings his faint
dancing windmills blotched birds of Holland
his drawer drawings nipple pulls his fish
drawings all lost the mantas sea snakes
syllables that startle drawings of what
he sees before he sees what he sees
what the drawer sees before it is drawn
open the dark under stone the sealed
passage murmur of crosshatchings
light floating up its wings bent wilted
little stuffed angels his bulb drawings
cellar-full and onions tulips radishes
shallots leeks dirt damp floors smoke
everywhere and in the air smoke*

*Along the dike marshes, the riverbank, blackbirds howling
from the windy reeds, Rembrandt has a limp
today – the mud smells like the wind, the wind
smells like shit, that flat land, baking and seeping,
trees breathing the farmhouses, growing like chimneys,
like toadstools, fat and distant, bloated with wind,
sun filling the wide spaces, shadow under the trees,
chiaroscuro, the ear hears first what is inside,
then the wind outside, begging, riddled with blackbirds,
sounds of wagons rolling, squeaking, echoes
of barrels rolling, falling apart, horses
with bells and music of pipes, flute, viols –
Rembrandt dancing – flurries from the dovecotes
like bells, falling in courses*

Young Man Pulling a Rope (Reprise)
Pen and brush, brown ink, heightened with white.
c. 1645

In pen and brush and folds
and bold outlines
and bristling
with the queer notion
that light has weight

and enough at that
to sound the bell
we cannot see
which at this moment
pours down

its pealing

―――

One small portfolio of pen and ink sketches by Rembrandt.
One ditto of shadow drawings and another of dancing windmills.
One ditto of blotched birds and another of howling blackbirds.
One large portfolio of drawings of the Tyrol drawn from nature by
    Roelant Savery.
One portfolio of drawings by various eminent masters.
One album in quarto containing sketches by Rembrandt.
One copy in Dutch of Albrecht Dürer's book on proportion with woodcuts.
One portfolio of engravings by Jan Lievens and Ferdinand Bol.
A few packets of sketches by Rembrandt as well as by others.
One stack of very large sheets of paper.
One box containing engravings by Hendrick Van Vliet after paintings
    by Rembrandt.

Saint Jerome beside a Pollard Willow
Etching with drypoint.
1648

Hold your right hand before you,
fingers touching thumb, wrist straight.
This is the willow stump
beginning an inch or so
below the wrist bone's bulge.

Now a tiny bird can perch on the thumbnail,
and from the top knuckle of the index finger,
a single willow branch can spray.
The rest is dark crosshatchings,
rather like a close-up view of human skin.

Jerome is an afterthought,
a bauble on a bracelet
with his skull and crucifix,
writing, writing –
while the lion, mostly behind the tree,

is waiting, waiting –
The willow grows by water,
and water, which does not fall with economy,
does in this background.
Smell of wet wood and damp lion,

the pen moving, its faint sound

*

*on the walls Rembrandt's smoke drawings
Rembrandt's flu Rembrandt's rheumatism
Rembrandt's Rembrandts the floor flat and swept
the wide and sorrowful boards through
the years it grows though he likes its right
side best, flares it like a feathered breast
oh nose, nose / he laments in the dark*

*Rembrandt's lost shadow drawings,
his faint dancing windmills, blotched
birds of Holland, all sold from the black folder,
his fish drawings, all lost, the mantas, sea snakes,
Geertje, Hendrickje, of that ménage, the less said –
syllables that startle, drawings of what, of what –
the less said – of what he sees before
he sees what he sees, what the drawer sees
before it is drawn open, the dark under stone,
the sealed passage, murmur of crosshatchings,
light floating up, its wings bent, wilted,*

Beggar Couple with Children and a Dog
Black chalk.
c. 1648

We're moving into this one,
the dog in the lead,
almost out of sight.

It's a passage,
and with their children
safe on their backs,

they've entered, too.
We're going to follow,
feeling warm as black chalk.

After taking this first step,
the dog pulls, but the cane steadies.
The next step is so inevitable

it never comes.

One folding screen covered in cloth.
One iron gorget.
One drawer in which there is a bird of paradise and six fans.
15 books of various sizes together with a quantity of black chalk.
One copy of a book in High German with prints of military figures.
Another book of the same with woodcuts.
One copy of a book in High German by Flavius Josephus profusely
 illustrated with copperplate engravings by Tobias Stimmer.
One old Bible with missing pages.
One small marble inkstand.
One death mask of Prince Maurice cast in plaster.

A Dog Lying on the Ground with a Collar around His Neck
Pen and brush in India ink.
c. 1648

Here is a compact dog, rather like a smudge,
especially along his spine,
where he might bristle before a fight.

But this dog is sleeping, his paws
drawn in almost like a cat, but without
the effect of neatness. Dog's limbs

are too long, won't tuck. One haunch
sticks up, he can't be comfortable.
Benesch catalogs him as a bear.

Perhaps his collar is too tight. His dreams
will wake him soon enough, and he'll be
in a bad mood. Bear or dog, it won't matter.

———

8. In the Foyer adjacent to the Gallery of Curios
    One painting of St. Joseph by Aert van Leyden.
    Three framed prints.
    One painting of the Annunciation.
    One small landscape painted from nature by Rembrandt.
    One small painting of a landscape by Hercules Seghers.
    One painting of the Descent from the Cross by Rembrandt.
    One head of a greyhound from life.

Christ Awakening the Apostles on the Mount of Olives

Pen and brush, brown ink.
c. 1648–49

Christ's in the center standing
in a robe that's left unshaded.
The darkness is all for Peter
who has been drawn over with sticky lines
as if wrapped by a prudent spider.
He's tangled in his dreams, can't attend.

The others are also slow to wake.
It's jagged where they are.
Their open eyes see nothing.
Christ says what he says. There's
a tree, a garden wall behind him,
figures stirring; these lines are drawn in haste.

———

One vanitas with a skull, retouched by Rembrandt.
One plaster statue of Diana Bathing by Adam van Vianen.
One study of a hunchback from life by Rembrandt.
One painting of three puppies from life by Titus van Rijn.
One sketch book of watercolors by the same.
One painting of the head of the Virgin Mary by the same.

The Singel in Amersfoort

Pen and bistre, wash.
c. 1648–50

    Here row houses climb toward our right
    from a chalky smudge of wash. Part
    of a tree grows from the frame.

    On the left nothing recognizable
    buttresses huge hatched trees. It's all
    wild, under construction. Still,

    it has managed to climb half out of
    the frame, now becomes a wall, a closer
    house, divided like a mind

    that's chosen to know itself
    only to a point, a place where neighbors
    politely don't stare in open windows.

———

One small painting of a landscape in the moonlight, retouched by Rembrandt.
One copy of a painting of the Scourging of Christ after the same.
One small nude study of a woman from life by the same.
One small unfinished landscape, lacking frogs, by the same.
One painting of a horse from life by the same.
One small painting by Dirck Hals.
One small painting of a fish from life.
One plaster basin with nude figures by Adam van Vianen.
One old trunk.
One old chest containing a quantity of red chalk.
Four chairs with black leather seats.
One pine table.

View across the IJ from the Diemen Dike
Pen and brush, brown ink, some white, on grayish paper.
c. 1649–50

Here is the calm of flat horizons,
church spire and village – almost as fine
as the paper's texture, a slow journey
for the quickest eye.

Three sailing vessels, one with a dinghy
moored behind, another moving to our right,
soon to pass behind the wash that fills
the dike. And this foreground, with waves

moving toward us, a slight wind bending
the reeds – it's not so fine,
not so careful, the lines are thick
or washed over, everything is moving.

In a moment when the wind picks up,
you can hear birds. You can't see them –
but there, in the reeds, listen –
where the waves won't die out –

―――

9. In the Small Studio for Rembrandt's Students
    In the First Bin.
Nothing but a quantity of smoke and dust.
    In the Second Bin.
Thirty-three ancient hand weapons, and wind instruments.
    In the Third Bin.
Sixty Indian hand weapons, arrows, shafts, javelins, and bows.
Thirteen bamboo pipes and flutes.
    In the Fourth Bin.
Thirteen arrows, bows, shields, etc.
    In the Fifth Bin.
A large collection of hands and heads cast in plaster from life
    together with a harp and a Turkish bow.

*

*ravening springs / silence takes a bite
running beside the fleeing moment whether
to suffocate or swallow hyena-like without
giving up its stride / still silence
oh nose of Rembrandt spilled from a beggar's bag
misshapen arse for air the cold the warm
in the nose it goes nobody minds a rhyme*

elegance of brocade sleeves, sprezzatura
*"I would ask my lord most kindly if he could see
to it that I might be paid as soon as possible
here in Amsterdam, and so through your kind
efforts on my behalf I should be able to enjoy
my pennies, and I shall remain eternally
grateful to you for all such acts of friendship."*

*Fifteen books only: the Bible, a Tacitus
an Ovid, perhaps Horace, Pliny . . .*

*A stuffed bird of paradise from New Guinea
from which the legs had been removed.
Rembrandt drew it with legs*

                              and without legs.

Winter Landscape
Pen and brush, brown ink.
c. 1649–50

Here nearest us, a fence
or a huge harp stands rootless.

Two brush strokes, longer
in the air than in this snow,

make what is neither near nor far
rise up, calm, and confront the eye.

Snow is the silence, untouched.
The farmhouse surrounds a few fine lines.

The near distance, the far storm,
the white snow where the brush poised

but did not touch.

In the Sixth Bin.
Seventeen hands and arms cast in plaster from life.
A collection of stag antlers.
Four sling weapons and longbows.
Five ancient helmets and shields.
Nine gourds and bottles.
Two sculptured heads portraying Barthel Beham and
 his wife cast in plaster.
One ancient Greek statue cast in plaster.
One marble bust of the Emperor Agrippa.
One marble bust of the Emperor Aurelius.
One study of Christ's head done from a model.
One Satyr's head with horns.

The Amstel Dike near Trompenburg
Pen and brush, brown ink, some white, on brown prepared paper.
c. 1649–50

The dike is a road which curves gently away.
A small sail near the horizon is darker
than the windmill, which must be more distant.

Nearer, on the right hand, a clump of trees
has almost become a forest, rare thing –
and it is the road, on which a tiny horse

approaches, that draws the eye – once there,
to play, perhaps, over the trees like a wind
(for it's always windy), then back, to where?

– the frame we carry everywhere – think of
that edge of thought, the book, the room,
the square windowpane, the eye's fading

periphery, the world's – somewhere between
a man's horizon and his soul, the line
he draws, and stays behind, over and again.

―――

One antique statue of a Sibyl.
One antique statue of Laocoön.
One large marine plant.
One marble bust of the Emperor Vitellius.
One marble bust of Seneca.
Three or four antique heads of women.
Another 4 heads (pigs' heads).
One small model of a metal cannon.
A collection of old textiles of various colors.
7 stringed instruments and a fish.
Two little pictures of squid by Rembrandt.

Farmhouses with a Water Mill amidst Trees
Pen and bistre, wash.
c. 1650

That trees design from the earth
a certain passage of air, of light,
shape it, toss it, he knew well –

That these little farms were stuck
on promontories where the trees would
by nature gather –

That they would join in a confluence
of seething shape with only
an old post, nearly dead,

poking up preposterously, yet
giving exact relief to that
amorphous sprawl –

So he gives us as much foreground as sky,
and both empty, gone quiet, ample space
opposite the dying tree

for a grazing cow and one
intensely distant windmill.

*old man in the mirror he sees who, who it is
that he paints each time until, the mirror covered
where have I gone / where
that slim youth with curly hair
a thousand faces he had all floating up
to air until this one now hanging
on the line waiting for the wind the air
to wring it dry dust it beat it with a broom
rub it on smooth stones kick it half inflated
into the sky and there like nothing else*

*– his bulb drawings, cellars-full, and onions,
tulips, radishes, shallots, leeks, dirt-damp
floors, smoke everywhere and in the air,
smoke on the walls, Rembrandt's smoke drawings
Rembrandt's flu, Rembrandt's rheumatism,
Rembrandt's Rembrandts, the floor flat and swept,
the wide and sorrowful boards.*

A Farmhouse among Trees
Pen and brush, brown ink, on buff paper.
c. 1650–51

It's an island
piled up by wind
and sun dazzle.

The woodpile leans
in a lee like a dinghy,
hiding snakes and centipedes.

There's no quiet behind the fence,
but in the densest trees,
where vision swirls, breaks,

and turns to foam,
there might be bare earth
shadowed by cool thorns,

a rabbit, pill bugs,
bird calls, wind worn,
but still no sound from the house.

―

10. In Rembrandt's Studio
    Twenty artifacts including halberds, swords and Indian fans.
    One set of costumes for an Indian man and woman.
    One giant's helmet.
    Five cuirasses.
    One wooden trumpet.
    One painting of two Moors by Rembrandt.
    One statue of a little child by Michelangelo.

A Lion Resting, Turned to the Left
Pen and brush.
c. 1650–52

The lion might speak,
holds his mouth as if,
however, he's chosen not to.

His great haunch
is an excuse for one
splendid sweep of brush.

His mane tangles to his eyes.
He's looking outward with disdain,
his rest disturbed.

There is something perhaps Chinese
beneath his forepaws,
a swirl, a mark. It is his.

———

11. On the Picture Rack
    One lion-skin and one lioness-skin, together with
        two fur garments.
    One large painting of Danae.
    One painting of a bittern from life by Rembrandt

Homer Reciting His Verses
Pen and brown ink.
1652

Here's a chance to draw a crowd,
not the baroque venereal blur
a goose quill might spill – but order itself –
listeners gather round – sit on the grass
if you must, but be drawn with a reed pen.

Where else should Homer be – dead center
in the blind spot for faintest stars,
and that he is, almost too faint to see,
blind Homer singing so long ago
to these jagged little hearts.

---

12. In the Small Office
    Ten paintings of various sizes by Rembrandt.
    One bedstead and a quantity of goose feathers.

*Through the years
it grows, though he likes its right side best,
flares it like a feathered breast. Oh nose,
nose, he laments, in the dark rubs his eyes,
squeezes them to see those yellow lights
flicker up like lightning bugs their little yellow
glowing butts – slow bubbles make on and off
murmur, being in equilibrium with dark,
swoop like minnows, hover and doubt at the tips
of grass they rise and tails flick from the meadow –
musical horses, their loose lips snort and twitch,
and the light almost meets from fire to fly,
and the glow suspends a blanket, Rembrandt's glow
drawings, chiaroscuro. Silence and darkness,
those old friends, old silence, silence the living
creature ravening springs – silence takes
a bite, running beside the fleeing moment –
wondering whether to suffocate or swallow
hyena-like, without giving up its stride,
still silence –*

The Washing of the Feet
Pen and brown ink.
c. 1653–55

Our feet bare, or nearly so,
and the earth always beneath us
until we change our roles –

It seems not only humble, but a peaceful
office, making once more
at end of day, that fine distinction,

dust on its way to dust, but
Christ crouches like an athlete.
He's scrubbed feet before.

There's work in the world to be done.
The disciple holds the arms
of his chair gingerly,

wishes this foot were not his,
he's working hard to play straight man,
wondering how well he'll come clean.

---

13. In the Basement Kitchen
    One pewter water jug.
    Several pots and pans.
    One small table.
    One cupboard.
    Several old chairs.
    Two chair cushions.

The Artist's Studio
Pen and two shades of brown ink, gray-brown wash,
a few corrections in white.
c. 1654

Here is the first floor studio and the window's upper half is bare
as is Hendrickje's, but a half dressed woman is not a nude.
There's a cradle on the table under the window, a newborn's,

Cornelia's – the first two Cornelias did not need one larger.
At left, the large easel is flimsy as a windmill, standing in
for the artist in his studio – the light is saved for Hendrickje

who may be warm in her seat by the fireplace – the room itself
seems warm with blocks of wash like square echoes of the window
panes drawn in calligraphic loops – Hendrickje's listening, but

to nothing he's saying – he's too busy getting all this down –
almost a domestic scene, almost a nude – though he's finished it,
no one will find it pleasing, so much more a portrait of a room

it is, than of a woman listening, her hand gripping the chair seat.
She knows better than to say she hasn't time for this – the light
is failing so rapidly – she can hear it in the sound of his reed pen.

---

14. In the Corridor
Nine white bowls.
Two earthenware dishes.

The Descent from the Cross by Torchlight
Etching and drypoint.
1654

A bird drops from tree to ground
in a single cursive gesture.
Light falls, waves subside.
But in descent, all motion dies.

Christ does not descend.
His body hangs in the arms
of the man facing away.
Light weighs upon him,

and from the dark that only
seems swarming up beneath,
a single hand is lit,
reaching toward the light.

---

15. Linen at the Laundry
Three men's shirts.
Six pocket handkerchiefs.
Twelve napkins.
Three tablecloths.
Several collars and cuffs.

*Oh nose, nose of Rembrandt,
spilled from a beggar's bag, misshapen arse
for air, for the cold, the warm, the shining webs
of light, and even the dark, in the nose
it goes, with spiders and rags and soot and coal,
there in the room with the mirror, and the rest:
the Roman medals, helmets, cuirasses, one gun
and one pistol, two gloves, one arbalest,
several walking sticks, the Raphael Madonna,
two gloves, one box full of minerals –
Oh nose, nose of Rembrandt, ancient hand weapons,
etchings, of Cranach, Raphael, Mantegna, Dürer,
Titian, thirty volumes of sketches by Rembrandt
himself – Oh nose, eyes, old face in the moon.*

Abraham's Sacrifice
Etching with drypoint.
1655

You've made up your mind,
faith, the knife in your hand.
But what if this moment doesn't come –
these angel wings like laundry
flapping in the wind?

Clean, white,
sweet smelling
angel wings flapping and rippling –
The wind they stir
you can feel in your beard –
There is nothing
so clean as angel wings,
nor so sharp
as your faith,
the knife in your hand.

Now, is this the moment?
The closest thing to white,
a cloud, stays far and wide,
its edges faint, fading,
and the only sound you hear,
farther yet,
is a distant crow.

Woman Looking out of a Window
Pen and brush, brown ink.
c. 1655–56

Down below us there's a street,
narrow and winding perhaps,
and the cobbles are guiding
small errant rivulets.

Children's voices ring like birds,
and she smiles slightly.
Perhaps there is a tree.
Why not? We can't disprove it.

We see only her resting form,
the window, square, a box of light,
something hanging on the wall –
Curtain? – made of such bold strokes,

it will not hold still.
Her dress billows into the calm
of dark brown ink. She'll wait
like this only a moment more.

---

16. In the First Attic Room
    Three bound bundles of reeds.
    Thirteen storks' legs.
    One large mirror with many fine runes.

A Coach
Pen and brush, brown ink.
c. 1655

This is a spidery contraption,
like a flying model
before the balsa hides in paper.

Without horses, it seems oddly
more a thing of function,
and the lines are fine but crowded.

Yet it's not all machine.
That one large rear wheel
is an egg, has no spokes to speak of,

must be dreaming of a solo flight,
bouncing down a hill away from the road,
while everything else drags to a halt.

———

One astrolabe of peculiar design.
One child's "fall-down hat."
A quantity of cloaks, mouse-nested.
One small mirror with cracks and fine runes.

The Skeleton Rider
Pen and brown ink.
c. 1655

Odd that the flesh should be so interesting,
or that bones, shy things,
can jumble so – one is enough for metaphor.

This rider holds a femur like a flag,
has one up his butt, how else to say –
Giving the horse reins was a droll idea.

Some bones are scrabbly as reed pens,
can't decide connections, go black as death.
The prancing horse is a skeleton, too.

The rider's leaning back as though
his skittery mount has pulled up short,
and dust from the road drifts through him.

---

17. In the Second Attic Room
    One large book of drawings of bones.
    Five pieces, comprising flutes in horn and ivory
    One small painting of Tobit with many birds by Rembrandt

    Done and inventoried on July 25 and 26, 1656

The Curator of the Insolvent Estate of Rembrandt van Rijn, Fine-Art Painter, has been authorized by Their Worships the Commissioners of Insolvency of this City to sell under Execution the requisitioned Graphic Art now remaining in the said Estate, consisting of Works of Art by various prominent Italian, French, German, and Netherlandish Masters which the said Rembrandt van Rijn has collected together with a great number of Curios. At the same time there will be sold a large collection of Drawings and Sketches by the said Rembrandt van Rijn himself. The Sale will take place on the day of the Year and at the hour stated above, at the house of Barent Janszoon Schuurman, Landlord of the Crown Imperial in the Kalverstraat, where the rest of this Property has been sold. Spread the word around.

A Girl Sleeping
Brush and brown ink.
c. 1655–56

There's as much chalk here
as might fly from fat moths
colliding in midair.

But sleeping, under her dreams,
she is a hand cupped in darkness,
none of it spilling out.

And if shapes matter –
something to kneel before,
to rest her head on,

as clearly isn't there
as the air she dreams of,
her cheek warm and invisible.

―

Spread the word around
turnips, fried onions, black bread
herring on a good day
spoons are a luxury
every room a step up or down
Spread the word around

Sleeping Woman at a Window
Reed pen and bistre.
c. 1655–57

It's not enough to see her,
her head resting against her right hand,
her left grasping the window sill.

We've got to look with her
across the street where a tree has just now
stopped shivering in a sudden breeze.

She meant to pause a moment from her work –
and the sill was so warm against her arm,
and that tree had just begun to stir.

―

Spread the word around
pewter for plates pots dishes ewers
sauce boats soup tureens tall mugs with lids
the pewter man is calling
anything leaking he'll melt down
the word around

Jael Driving a Nail into the Head of Sisera

Pen and bistre, white body color.
c. 1657–60

Get the picture: mallet and railroad spike,
backswing a little over the top,
but plenty of room for a sweeping stroke.

Her head's down. It's all balanced.
She's not going to miss. Sisera's cumbency
is brilliant. Everything is to the point

except perhaps a background table leg.
It's all so neat, so concentrated,
but in a moment it will be less so.

=

peat burns slow
spread the word
wooden plates and dishes
only the poor
the fork is a gleam in time's eye
spread the word
burns slow

Christ and the Woman Taken in Adultery
Pen and brush, brown ink.
c. 1659–60

Soo jachtig om Christus in zijn antwoordt te verschalken,
konden zij 't schrifterlick antwoordt niet afwachten.

(So eager to ensnare Christ in his own reply,
the scribes could not wait for the answer.)

(Inscription in Rembrandt's own hand
on a strip of paper attached below.)

"Soo jachtig" – all the world crowds in a crowd.
Christ stands near the center, both
his hands almost drawn.

Then toward his right, his left, his children
shade darker toward the frame – lines
that show us where they stand grow

broad as bricks – thus we wait, *soo jachtig,*
for the words which already draw
a rush of unbidden light.

---

olipotrigo
capon lamb beef sausage
pig's head, trotters
sheep's trotters
artichokes and spices
egg yolks, sour wine and butter
the word
served with chestnuts

potatoes and tomatoes are poisonous
words

Self-Portrait at an Easel
Oil on canvas.
1660

All that mugging in the etchings
has come to this, in brown and black.
The old man, eyebrows raised,

that question in the eyes
grown near bursting.

Last summer's weeds swaying in a field,
their empty pods, their blossoms dried,
windmill on the faint and far horizon,

trees clumped like that nose
and lost to sun and wind –

Old man looking at himself,
and having got it nearly right,
puts down his brush –

before he covers the mirror,
can't resist making one last face.

―

A flock of words

Self-Portrait as Saint Paul
Oil on canvas.
1661

You can almost tell what he's thinking,
looking back toward us and that benison
of light made plausible by white lead

scratched into his headdress – forehead,
cheek, drooping nose, lit by it – his
head turns toward us in smaller increments

than the brushstrokes of his hair and
we see it's all some kind of question:
those eyebrows – *both of them* – at first

we noticed only the one nearest the light,
arched, and the forehead roughly
furrowed – he's turned away from that thing

he was reading, the words almost… just past
the grip of his right hand. It's something
of a joke, and we know it, too, but have

forgotten, and that's why the sadness,
the lips below that ghost mustache too
firm for forgiveness, and despite the light,

it's all fading – before it was so close,
so near – the law, the truth, something
a sinner might hope to hope for.

*

*In 1662 sold Saskia's grave in the chancel
behind the organ – three gravediggers
scraped out Saskia's bones to make room
for the next customer, Hillegondt Willems –
Hendrickje of plague in 1663, rented
a grave unmarked in Westerkerk 10
guilder and 13 stuivers*

*The paint itself usually linseed oil,
sometimes walnut which yellows less
heated to vary viscosity and with breadcrumbs,
urine, the pigments ground with a muller
on a grinding slab – a small amount of egg yolk*

brushed, knifed, smeared, a sweet girl

*Eight months after his marriage to Hiskia van Loo,
Titus of the plague (1668) buried
also in a rented grave in Westerkerk*

*Thixotropy – a rheological phenomenon:
reversible change from a set gel-like
condition of a plastic material under the influence
of some mechanical force – a brush*

brushed, knifed, smeared,

―――

*October 5, 1669,
a dead man*

Self-Portrait with Brushes, Maulstick, and Palette in Hand
Oil on canvas.
1662

Here is the master painting himself,
and this one is not so much seeing
as painting.

All that gear is a blur thrust forward.
His cap is one white gash of lead,
but steady

over that still and stern visage.
Scratched loops meander at the collar.
His curly hair

suggests a damp day, but behind
him on the lit wall he's drawn,
freehand, of course,

two fine circles, big as a man,
of the kind Giotto drew for Cimabue,
and Dante praised,

but they reach outside the frame.
In the midst of that *sprezzatura*,
loose strokes, *lossigheid*,

he's made those two fine circles
and now thrusts out the brush,
his head still,

everything else a flushed covey
of meadow birds, flurry and panic –
The circles,

he says, you finish them – the
maulstick pokes you in the chest
until you step back

or blink.

Self-Portrait in a Turban
Oil on canvas.
1669

Still playing with costumes,
he's made the turban balance
the sagging face – tried it higher
than it is, in fact.

There's more hair in this last view,
a cloud of gray, and this is still
his favorite side – his right eye
in the light,

left lurking in the dark behind
that nose now more like
a plowed field, scratched
and pocked, yet milder –
peaceful, in fact.

There's more of the double chin,
and the cheek, too, is resigned –
but the paint of the turban
and at the V of the neck
is still violent.

At first he looks like a woman –
that is the peaceful part,
the settling – then the light
changes – one of us has moved
closer,

and we can see the eye painted
astonishingly – the brush slowed,
breath held, time stopped one
last time.

*

*Old man in the mirror, sitting today in the room
with the robes and hats with feathers, he sees the ghost,
each time and then each time, the face, the eyes,
until, the mirror covered again, the nose,
where have I gone, where, that slim youth
with curly hair, a thousand faces he had
all floating up to air, until this one.*

*Bells, falling in courses
like flurries from dovecotes*

―――

word, the last

Self-Portrait as Democritus
Oil on canvas.
Lost

Here in the year of his death, he's done himself
in the rough tone of The Slaughtered Ox, a cheerful geezer,
his toothless mirth dissolving into the white noise

that saturates this black canvas – he'll not die of it,
this laughter, but he's fading under his glowing cap.
There's a figure, a bust, behind him, so he's in

his studio tarnishing himself, what better word?
the plague has taken Titus to a rented grave –
Time's running out – nothing cuts like an old saw –

Democritus is said to have put out his eyes
in order that he might avoid outside disturbance,
not such a cheerful way to guard his thoughts –

better, perhaps, to draw the curtain, welcome
the dark from which a few more images may spill,
among them the joke for which there is no laughter,

fit for this laughter, for which there is no joke.

———

last

Self-Portrait, Hands Clasped
Oil on canvas.
1669

Is this the last, we wonder –
the face sags and the nose grows,
an old pumpkin rotting in a trash heap.

The sleeve and arm where he used to flourish
so much virtuosity is gloom itself –
doodverf, his dead color.

He's changed his mind about the hands
and painted out the brush –
they are clasped tightly, like his lips.

Look what he's found in the mirror's maw,
under his eyes, the folds failing,
the pitted cheek –

but his collar and his hair crawl
with strange light,
and the eyes, not sunken,

see and decide – this, then.
One last reflecting dab
for the nose –

princely.

*

*Now it's lost in the moon, stags' horns,
the rare cups of Venetian glass, the bird
of paradise, there in the moon, there
on the far horizon, faint as a windmill.
Now it's hanging on the line, waiting
for the wind, the air, to wring it dry, dust it,
beat it with a broom, rub it on smooth stones,
kick it half inflated into the sky,
and there like nothing else, begin to sing,
floating inside the dark, the rushing wind,
all the noise of an angel hovering.*

List of Acknowledgements

The Beloit Poetry Journal: "The Rat Poison Peddler," "Twenty Self Portraits," "Christ Awakening the Apostles," and "Abraham's Sacrifice."

College English: "Portrait of Saskia in a Straw Hat," "The Skeleton Rider," "Christ Walking on the Waves," "The Washing of the Feet," "Jacob and Rachael Listening to an Account of Joseph's Dreams," "The Good Samaritan Arriving at the Inn," and "Homer Reciting his Verses."

The Cumberland Poetry Review: "The Amstel Dike," and "A Coach."

ELF: "Portrait of Maria Trip."

The Florida Review: "Woman with a Child Frightened by a Dog."

Hanging Loose: "Woman in North Holland Costume," and "Beggar Couple with Children and a Dog," and "Rembrandt's Nose."

Interim: "The Singel in Amersfoort."

The Laurel Review: "Seated Old Woman in a Large Head-dress," and "Portrait Bust of a Lady in a Cap."

The Literary Review: "A Lion Resting."

The Marlboro Review: "The Entombment, Over a Sketch of an Executioner."

Sewanee Review: "Woman Seated in an Armchair," "Woman Leaning Out of a Window," "Winter Landscape," "Judas Returning the Thirty Pieces of Silver," and "Three Women Looking Out from an Open Door."

Sonora Review: "Hendrikje in the Artist's Studio."

TriQuarterly: "The Naughty Child," "Standing Beggar," and "Saskia Sitting up in Bed."

West Branch: "Old Man with his Arms Extended," "Study for an Adoration of the Maji," and "Christ and the Woman Taken in Adultery."

Resources

Books

Bailey, Anthony. *Rembrandt's House: Exploring the World of the Great Master.* New York: Tauris Parke Paperbacks, 2014.

Burnet, John. *Rembrandt and His Works.* London: D. Bogue, 1849.

Crenshaw, Paul. *Rembrandt's Bankruptcy: The Artist, His Patrons, and the Art Market in Seventeenth-Century Netherlands.* Cambridge: Cambridge University Press, 2006.

Golahny, Amy. *Rembrandt's Reading: The Artist's Bookshelf of Ancient Poetry and History.* Amsterdam: Amsterdam University Press, 2003.

Haak, Bob. *Rembrandt's Drawings.* Translated by Elizabeth Willems-Treeman. Woodstock, N.Y.: Overlook Press, 1976.

Rembrandt van Rijn. *Drawings of Rembrandt: With a Selection of Drawing by His Pupils and Followers.* With an Introduction, Commentary, and Supplementary Material by Seymour Slive. 2 vols. New York: Dover Publications, 1965.

Rembrandt van Rijn. *The Complete Etchings of Rembrandt: Reproduced in Original Size.* Edited by Gary Schwartz. New York: Dover Publications, 1988.

Schama, Simon. *Rembrandt's Eyes.* New York: Penguin Books, 2014.

Smith, John. *A Catalogue Raisonné of the Works of the Most Eminent Dutch Painters of the Seventeenth Century. . ., Volume 7.* London: Smith and Son, 1837.

Strauss, Walter L., and Marjon van der Meulen. *The Rembrandt Documents.* With the assistance of S.A.C. Dudok van Heel and P.J.M. de Baar. New York: Abaris Books, 1979.

Wetering, Ernst van de. *Rembrandt: The Painter at Work.* Amsterdam: Amsterdam University Press, 1997

Electronic

https://en.wikipedia.org/wiki/List_of_drawings_by_Rembrandt

https://en.wikipedia.org/wiki/List_of_etchings_by_Rembrandt

https://en.wikipedia.org/wiki/List_of_paintings_by_Rembrandt

http://remdoc.huygens.knaw.nl (The original Dutch inventory with its English translation.)

Institutions

Ashmolean Museum, Oxford.

Frick Collection, New York.

Museum Het Rembrandthuis (Rembrandt House), Amsterdam.

Rijksmuseum, Amsterdam.

About the Author

Charles Wyatt is the author of two collections of short fiction, (*Listening to Mozart*, University of Iowa Press, *Swan of Tuonela*, Hanging Loose Press), a novella (*Falling Stones: the Spirit Autobiography of S.M. Jones*, Texas Review Press), and three poetry chapbooks (*A Girl Sleeping*, Sow's Ear Poetry Review Chapbook Series, *Myomancy*, Finishing Line Press,  *Angelicus ex Machina*, Finishing Line Press). He is the recipient of the Beloit Poetry Journal's 2010 Chad Walsh Prize and the Writers at Work 2013 Fellowship in Poetry. A poetry collection, *Goldberg-Variations*, was published by Carolina Wren Press in 2015.

A graduate of the Curtis Institute of Music (BM), The Philadelphia Musical Academy (MM), and Warren Wilson College (MFA), he has served as visiting writer at Binghamton University, Denison University, The University of Central Oklahoma, Purdue University, and Oberlin College. He currently teaches in the Low Residency Program of the University of Nebraska Omaha and the Writing Program of UCLA Extension. He was previously principal flutist of the Nashville Symphony for 25 years. Learn more:

www.charleswyatt.com ; www.facebook.com/charlesmwyatt

© Photo credit: Clark Thomas

www.ingramcontent.com/pod-product-compliance
Lightning Source LLC
Chambersburg PA
CBHW042325150426
43192CB00004B/122